GHOST DANCE

Gregory O'Donoghue

ACKNOWLEDGEMENTS

Acknowledgements are due to the editors of *Exile* (Toronto), *Poetry Ireland Review*, *Poetry London*, *Poets of Munster*, *The SHop*, *Southward*, *Quarry* (Kingston Ont.). 'Ithaca' first appeared, translated into Spanish by Martín Veiga and David MacKenzie, in *Raiceir e Vento* (2003). 'The Permanent Way' first appeared as title poem in a chapbook from Three Spires Press. 'Searching for an Answer' first appeared in its present form in *A Visit to the Clockmaker* (Kristin Dimitrova/Gregory O'Donoghue, Southward Editions, 2005). 'Dusky Curls' is partly indebted to a version by E. Powys Mathers. 'On the Star Fort Elizabeth' was first aired in the movie *In the Hands of Erato*. Some of these poems were broadcast on Lyric FM. Special thanks to Thomas McCarthy who scrutinised the penultimate typescript. I am grateful to Cork City Council for an artist's bursary awarded in 2004.

For Patrick Galvin

Contents

Brainse Dhromchonnrach
Drumcondra Branch
Tel. 8377296

Foreword by Maurice Riordan   i

Charms   *1*

PART ONE

The Permanent Way   5
Ithaca   6
Fable of Three Surgeons   9
Blow-in   11
Symbols   13
Spiritual Body-Snatching   14
Newspaper   15
Fate   16
Playing with Numbers   18
Only a Dream   21
Emily Jane Brontë   23
Anna Akhmatova   25
Grandma's Fairytales   26

PART TWO

On the Star Fort Elizabeth   31
Driftwood   33
Aquarium   35
Masks   36
Bourbon   37
Lullaby   38
Between the Lines   39
Moving On   41

I wake to sleep, and take my waking slow.
I feel my fate in which I cannot fear.
I learn by going where I have to go.

— Theodore Roethke

Foreword
by Maurice Riordan

Shortly after the last time I met Gregory O'Donoghue (in June 2005), he sent me a copy of 'A Sofia Notebook', the touching melancholy love-sequence that ends this posthumous collection of his poems. It was accompanied by a handwritten note – an actual *Go Raibh Maith Agat* card which he must have bought in Eason's. I now believe this unexpected gesture was valedictory – that the note as well as the 'Notebook' were meant as a final act of sharing and friendship.

We went back a long way. Gregory O'Donoghue was part of that talented generation at University College Cork when I went there in 1970. Among them were Michael Davitt, Nuala Ní Dhomhnaill, Patrick Crotty, and later they were joined by Thomas McCarthy, Theo Dorgan, Seán Dunne, Gerry Murphy and Greg Delanty. UCC was an unusually hospitable nursery for poets in the 70s. The place was overcrowded, the library was almost unusable, and the lectures were seldom worth going to. But among the staff in the Irish and English departments were the poets Seán Ó Ríordáin, John Montague, Seán Ó Tuama and Sean Lucy. And Paul Durcan was there too studying archaeology and history. An unofficial education was on offer in the cafeterias and the city's pubs.

Gregory was already a conspicuous presence in that scene, perched most nights at the bar in *The Long Valley*. He had read Pound and Berryman intensely. Robert Graves would later join them among his heroes, though it was the mythography more than the poems that he admired. After that his tastes did not change significantly. Something of Pound's lyrical phrasing remained part of his music. And Berryman's wayward disordered imagination runs as a background programme to his work. When he finished 'A Sofia Notebook', he told me he remembered the last line of the Sonnets: 'and every word that I have gasped of you is true.'

Later I would get to know Greg well in Canada, where he had gone (with his first wife, Fiona Walton) to do a Ph.D. at Queen's in

Kingston, Ontario, while I was down the road at McMaster in Hamilton. He enjoyed the wide reading demanded by the course, but he was, understandably, daunted by the prospect of writing academic papers. We continued our informal education, many long afternoons in the less reputable taverns of Hamilton and Kingston. And we made several Greyhound bus trips over the border to similar establishments in New York, Washington, Penn State, and to Boston, where we would stay on Park Street with his friend Robert Perkins.

That first spell in Canada was a good one for Greg. He was accumulating the basis for a collection to follow his first book *Kicking*, which had been published by Peter Fallon's Gallery Press in 1975. Eleven new poems appeared in *Exile,* among them his fine poem 'Anna Akhmatova' collected here; 'Aquarium' also dates from that time, inspired by the only item of personal property I knew him to be devoted to.

Later I grew from under his shadow, acquiring my own strong preferences about poems. But it was hard to get the better of Greg in an argument – and not only about poetry. When he was living in Grantham (where he had moved with his Canadian wife, Gail Savoy), I remember us walking beside the river and for some reason disagreeing about which way it was flowing. I was pretty sure it flowed north, but Greg was adamant. I was vindicated when we came to a weir. Greg looked inquiringly at the water for a long time before he conceded that, yes, the river *must* be flowing down *over* the weir.

On other occasions he would come down to stay with us in London. Greg was not always the most conventional house guest. When he'd emerge into daylight after a heavy night, if you offered him breakfast, he might ask with a raised eyebrow, "Is there a beer in the fridge?" One morning he left our flat in Earls Court to buy croissants. And that was that – until a couple of hours later when the police knocked on the door. An 'uncooperative individual' had been found in the street with a letter addressed to me in his pocket. Greg had been nicked!

But he was good to have in the house. By now I had children, and, while the domestic routine continued, the hours were spent thumbing through volumes of poems, quoting, recollecting, drawing attention, assessing – always at an exacting level of attention and discussion. Even so, Greg — though no babysitter — was ever generous and gentle with the children, his spirit one that was enhanced by their presence.

That gentleness of spirit was a quality that grew as he got older. I was glad when he returned to Cork, where he found himself, perhaps to his surprise, appreciated by younger poets, and for the first time supported as a writer. More importantly, his poems began to come again, and I think with a greater fluency than before.

Many of the poems in this volume are the result of that flourishing. I can only read them now with a sad awareness of what might have followed, of the poems he could be writing and sending to me for years to come. But I'm aware too he did not forsee old age. He was sensitive to the preternatural and the ghostly presences, and had a strong sense of fatality. He tended to view himself in the tradition of the *poetes maudits*. But these poems have as well a wry and understated sense of reconciliation with the melancholy outcome of our lives and loves. Thinking of their spare exquisite expression, I am reminded of the lines that end 'Four A.M.':

> how the Japanese
> in their painting use rain so quietly
> it's like a downpouring of light.

*

Twenty-nine years ago, a Greyhound bus climbing out of Harrisburg, Pennsylvania, behind us a view of the Susquehanna River and beyond the Blue Mountains lapped in misty sunshine. We're on one of our escapades and it's early morning. Even so Greg takes out the hip-flask, wrapped as I see it now in an indigo shammy-cloth. "Have a swig," he says, "go on." And citing the 'Tailor' Buckley: "The world's only a blue bag. Knock a squeeze out it while you can!" Friend, you did – and you have left us the gift of your late excellence. *Go raibh maith agat.*

iii

Charms

I am humming
huddling through rain

going about my business
until I'm flapped at

by someone well-dressed,
a tweedy thrush in distress.

Up-close, she is a smile
as she hands me a booklet

and a pendant
on a pale blue ribbon:

a Miraculous Medal.

*

I am reminded
of coming off the bus at twilight

in drizzle in Lafayette:
voodoo woman insisting I take

a mojo on my journey—
same words as tonight

"It will do you no harm."

The small pouch pressed into my palm
was light with I don't know what —

whisker of a catfish,
pebble from the bayou,

powdered chicken leg,

chip of onyx
off a rich man's tomb—

Ah life, a Lucky Bag!

PART ONE

The Permanent Way

Protesting from moon-washed loops and sidings,
trailing their triple-lanterned brakevans,

unlovely trains of railflats, hoppers, cranes,
rattle through the darkness to converge

where the work is: roads to be uprooted,
restrictive curves widened, bridges raised.

Interchangeable to the guard who
yards back from the working train, uncouples,

screws down the brakevan. Feeds his cast-iron fire,
fastens both veranda doors and settles

in cramped sleep; or plays his handlamp over
a book concealed among the books of rules;

or, high summer perhaps, wanders the track
thinking aloud to shapes the bushes make.

But when the snow is thick or the rain chill
he has visitors: one by one, men come,

cluster at the stove, story-telling, cursing.
"Our brawn, men like us!" Roving railroad gangs

through the decades: the tale of some spent platelayer
for every rocked sleeper these roads run over.

Ithaca
on reading Anton Avilés de Taramancos

1

From Ilium's torched towers
Weary Odysseus
On the godly sea

Ten-year lost weekend
Of rosy-fingered dawns
Spectacular run of near-disasters

Crew metamorphosed to swine
Blood roaring fiercely
To sirens' sweet soul music

No surprise uxorious Odysseus
Sings when bundled back
Into his native cove

Although again and again
Breaking his tune to howl
Salt and exile from his bones

A noise unimaginable
Last wolf howling
At the world's last sundown

Yet he is home and dry
When Eurycleia
Who scrubbed him as a child

Bathes him head to toe
Cries *O mercy*
Knowing him by his boyhood scar

And his deaf-blind mangy dog Argos
Who waited twenty years
Can now go happily to Hades

2

Avilés de Taramancos
Exiled nearly twenty years

To Colombia with a diploma
In nautical studies

Where like a dog hoarding
Digging up a bone

Your verse over and again
Scrabbled at natal ground

Small wonder
You wrote a poem 'Ithaca'

An old deaf dog the only
Caress of happiness

Symbol of childhood
"Symbol of childhood"

Version of Ithaca
Her shifting metaphors

Various as the myriad notions
Travellers have of home

Hold-all for the visions
Of the cursed or blest

Even for those audacious
Enough to dream a night

Prophesying in pillowtalk
To some shrewd Penelope.

Fable of Three Surgeons

One

from Saskatchewan
who knitted severed fingers

back on a piano-player
who, a month later,

tickled the ivories
at Carnegie Hall.

Two

stitched legs
back on a Seattle man

who then almost won
the New York marathon.

Three

lectured on
expertise picked up

in the great Lone Star State:
his amputee a cowboy

on alcohol and cocaine
who spurred his horse

at the Santa Fé freight train—
flew through the middle of the air,

bounced off a nodding donkey,
fell into an oil well;

the surgeon knitted back
all that remained—

a horse's ass and a Stetson hat;
his patient ruins pianos, can't run;

but don't picnic today
on the White House lawn.

Blow-in
i.m. Seán Dunne 1956-1995

I miss your voice sizzling
brimstone on the phone
"That shite editor...!"

Blow-in tyro from Waterford
steadily taking Cork's measure—

you strolled an afternoon
into the eve of World War II
with the ghost of Elizabeth Bowen,

watched the heron
curled initial on vellum
in the swamplands of the Gearagh,

shimmer of red admirals
on byroads between
Ballyvourney and Ballymakeera

while weighing the fish of Thomas Merton,
the berries of Anna Akhmatova.

I have given up doubt.
that old. worn-out coat...

Seán, I have not—
up pop goblins in their best suits:
life is fettered to doubt...

In August a procession
coiled westward through the heat.

11

rolling valleys lit with purple scarlet
lanterns of fuchsia,

past the goddess Gobnait's holy well,
her fertility bees,

to your grave in the Cúil Aodha
of Seán Ó Riordáin, Seán Ó Riada.

Symbols

Candle of seven tines
beside an outsize
radiant guitar-playing
doll mechanical Santa Claus;

a pagan
at a loss to imagine
what the window-dresser
is dreaming, I know this place—

its hopeless
ignorance, know with every census
it votes itself a Christian city;
its people use phrases

like 'King of the Jews'
in the same breath as
'Our Lord'...
                    "Our Lord"?
the words mean

Our guardian of the loaf
just as 'Our Lady' translates
Our kneader of the loaf—
for "King of the Jews"

ask a Jew...
Seven-branched candelabra
in a department store window
selling Christmas.

Spiritual Body-Snatching

Why bring flowers to a funeral,
the dead can't scent them—
or is it as other rituals
a comfort to the living
like spiritual body-snatching?

A corpse who in its time
refused to darken the door
of church, kirk or chapel
being prayed for in the drizzle,
lowered down to words

he'd long thought meaningless—
the grain of his life altered
by a blind mouth
"We know by how he lived
he was, in spirit, Christian!"

He was a devout heathen
steadfast to his last breath...
yards from the coffin
his last mistress and her siblings—
three weird sisters scrying.

Newspaper

Predictable day, predictable as
the righteous xenophobe who prefaces
paragraphs with "I am not a racist."

A day original as the disgraced
politician who gets true religion,
writes a best-seller on his conversion.

And more fool I to let it get to me—
day of ditchwater to disappear from,
become a drifter like Abraham-man—

vagabond of the 16th century
when bishops couldn't tell if the Abram
was lunatic or feigning lunacy.

Fate

Standing in the street,
heat on the city—
seaside weather—

I could sit
inside the pub
if definite

this is the one
where we agreed to meet—
my friends are known

for turning up late;
I cool my heels,
invent stories,

play with
numbers—
Five, what's Five

in Tarot?
Five, also called
Gospel:

a naked woman
holds an
olive twig,

the snake bites
its own tail
for happiness:

religious blindness
shall pass,
you will survive...

I knew a time
when someone died
every mirror

would be shawled,
every clock
in the house

stopped
on the very stroke
of the minute...

Only an hour late
they arrive
out of breath—

been to see
·a solicitor,
drafted a Will:

these people,
fitter and younger,
hearing a clock tick.

Playing with Numbers
Wyrd bith ful araed

Seven

She tries to read me,
turns up Seven,
the Snake—

I know she has not
the gift,
is guessing.

I translate
Seven
to myself:

someone is
quarter confused,
three-quarters

his own
worst enemy—
crocodiles, baby

vultures,
bad omens:
betrayal—

a girlfriend
will leave
with all the money.

Fourteen

Eve,
Vale of Tears:
she will elope

with a married man
who will leave
after seven years—

she will stalk him,
knife him,
torch his house.

Eleven

King David's card
of dominance—
your enemies are duped,

their princes
piss themselves:
Josephine drew this

for Napoleon
on the eve of the battle
of Austerlitz.

Six

The Sky...
If the sun faces up
prepare to believe

in love at first sight.
If the moon,
it will happen

in a ballroom
or by a garden wall
close on midnight.

Only a Dream

You believe
things like me
are fiction:

pronounce
the word—
does not rhyme

with spire,
rhymes with peer—
vampeer.

I can safely
tell you this
in the knowledge

you still will think
things like me
do not exist—

as to your Tarot:
turn any card
with your left hand—

you draw
Thirteen, High Priest:
you will marry

war and deceit,
nights of grief—
your best friend,

your confidant,
will skedaddle
with the fickle

woman you still
love— don't worry,
I have lived

many shambolic
thousands of years,
will be around

to put
you out
of your misery.

Emily Jane Brontë

I'll walk where my own nature would be leading:
It vexes me to choose another guide...
—*'Stanza'*

A single building on the skyline,
the Parsonage blue and bleak:

home from your home—
every breeze

that whirls the wildering drift—
moor-rambler.

When Crow Hill
erupted in columns of boulders

and mud from every bit of bog
you were all of six years.

Your sisters and brother
ran for shelter; you dove under

the red wing of the storm,
your drenched

long legs doing a dance:
first pagan on the planet.

You puzzled
your benign Irish father:

My lover is the west wind...
he for whom I wait

23

thus ever comes to me.
You puzzled

the kitchen maid with
I am heath.

Your sister Charlotte
could not understand,

burned your notebooks...
a promising curate on her mind

as she struck out stanzas
and adverbs from your poems

then—"suffering from sacrilege"—
cried herself to sleep for weeks.

Anna Akhmatova
after her Requiem

Another anniversary; I hear you
dragged to the window, your dead

heels across the floorboards;
again you shake your beautiful head

and say: "Coming here is coming home."
I can't remember all their names,

the marvellous books are burned:
for them I have stitched a wide shroud

from their own words; I will never
forget them, even if my mouth is broken.

Do not build a memorial to me
near the sea where I was born;

nor in Tsarsky Sad by the sacred stump
where an inconsolate ghost calls me;

build it here by the broken door
that even in death I will remember

the horror of the Black Marias;
here where an old woman yelped

like a kicked pup— let the snow thaw
in streams from my bronze eyelids,

let the prison dove call,
and the boats go quietly in the mist.

Grandma's Fairytales

When you died
I was that young
I half imagined

it was all
just a spell:
your story

only
in its middle—
an enchanted sleep.

Tonight
in a cloak of cloud—
milky blue

as inside
a mussel shell—
the new moon

polishes
the stone jar
that was

her grandmother's
last
gift to her:

Queen Meg's
swoon cream,
the flying

cream of witches,
milky way
of the left-hand path,

the miracle
ointment
rubbed on naked

to glimpse
the Scroll of Life
unless it kills

outright
from splashing
on a birthmark.

Or—*Once upon*
a time, a very
good time it was

Or—*Beware the one*
with a heart of stone,
eyes of wood

Or—*When you meet*
a beautiful woman
don't be shy,

just say "May I style
you pretty Molly O"
you never know.

The night
before your funeral,
as I stood alone

beside you in vigil,
two memories:
how you always

ended your ghost stories
on the same
rhyme

I had a little awl
I stuck it in the wall
and that's all

and the pair of us
upstairs
on a double-decker bus,

front window seats,
off to see
the wonderful *Wizard of Oz.*

PART TWO

On the Star Fort Elizabeth

We pass
(no shebeen this) Ireland's
oldest licensed premises,

barely glance
at the plaque that says
the Dukes of Wellington

and Marlborough drank here.
We are going to stand upon
the northeast limb of a star.

Wellington, Arthur Wellesley,
never was at ease
with his Irish nativity:

"Of course,
Sir, to be born in a stable
does not make one a horse."

We stroll a rock solid star
that might have grown from the ground;
our gazes for each other

yet also over the parapet
at Shandon; the summits
of the river valley; the sun-warmed limestone.

Your arm crooked through my elbow
is where we stand
however ambiguously we feel

about this fort,
its antennae in five directions.
We'd not want

to lurch along Barrack Street
singing tribal songs of a Saturday night—
beamed in and thumbed,

our signatures
to our confessions
written with fishbones.

Arthur Wellesley
was not a cut of beef in a boot,
nor was he a horse,

nor—born in a stable—the Christ.
We'll come down off this planet.
Have a squeeze and slow kiss first.

Driftwood

Sloughing reverie
I pile more coal on the fire
thinking I'd rather be

away in Lafayette
throwing snake-eyes for quits,
instead of pausing

to admire
our serpent,
our sculpture trouvé—

we'd been striding
into the wind on Long Strand

where you chose stones
for their fossil patternings

and I for flattened roundness,
weight to skim across
troughs beneath the snaking breakers.

Far along we saw a hare
yet, in focus, the hare
was a python

whorled in waterlogged driftwood—
a spiral of grained and woven
browns, dulled greys, golds.

I took its midriff,
you its neck;
we swopped holds

crossing the marram grass
until it sat
in the boot of the car

travelling towards the quarrel
that made you pack
your bags forever.

Only coincidence,
still—I eye our snake:
it's enough to make

anyone superstitious.
We'd been in Eden,
Stolen the evidence.

Aquarium

I am a woman on the land,
I am a selkie in the sea. (Trad.)

I build a minute world
of filters, coloured rocks
and long fern weeds
for guppies, minnowy swordtails,

the ink-black molly;
clean it for the angels
who on fanned fins and threads
glide awed mucous mouths

to procreate in a kiss:
creation stilled to an eye,
seasonless Paradiso,
the great fish summoned at will

or dismissed— Ahab's
breaching monster!
and remember at ease
Boston's great cylinder

of wistful eels,
blunt snookered sharks
gliding back from the glass—
by the sway of the moray

I conjured the green scales
of a selkie at the chapel door
and heard desire return
in cries, the keen of seals.

Masks

Her frown sends you to an arid place—
think desert, think Arizona,
shoot your horse and yourself:
here are bleached cattle skulls,
scent of ambush on the wind.

Seeing her smile dissolves
time and space— you could be
in medieval Spain, France, Italy,
among people who believe eyes
are windows to the soul—
her soul seems fetching.

Most strange of all
her open honest face
when she is practising deceit—
possibly her untruths are nothing
to lies she constantly
tells her heart.

There is another face she wears
when thinking matters over...
I have seen too many layers
of masks, have ceased to care or wonder
what face she sees before her mirror.

Bourbon

You don't just drop in to escape the snow.
There are half-decent places up the street,
anywhere's less a dive than this deadbeat
hole-in-the-wall in South Ontario.

You sit at ease although you don't belong
and drink bourbon with the kind of woman
who last tried daylight before Solomon
sloped into the rhythms of his first Song.

Charcoal-filtered smoky Jack D,
Old No.7 out of Tennessee's
limestone springs and rickyards of hickory—
I'm not swimming in misery or strife,
just vacant tippling to jukebox ditties
about lost women, the wild side of life.

Lullaby

O she said from the blue without mercy
"You give me the creeps, your smile's sort of sly,
Now take your old claw away from my knee,

"I'd rather eat mice and live in a tree
Than be rocked to sleep by your lullaby"—
So she said from the blue without mercy.

"I'd rather go live in some nunnery
To be scourged by demons until I die,
Now take your old claw away from my knee,

"Parcel yourself, your pet snake and goatee,
Inside your manky coat and say goodbye"—
So she said from the blue without mercy.

"If you're the last man I'll go die lonely
And dance across star-frost behind the sky.
Now take your old claw away from my knee."

I thought, in truth, she wanted me only—
Was hungry like me, just a little shy;
But she said from the blue without mercy
"Ah take your old claw away from my knee."

Between the Lines

Perhaps she has not
choreographed
this meeting to avoid

anything more intimate
than holding hands?
She hauls me to view

plastic wreaths, pots, pans,
belt-buckles,
market-stall pottery;

her chat seems full
of marginal matters, small
as mice in wheat-fields

until her mind's eye swoops,
kestrel's embrace;
yet it is talk salted with hints—

her workload will increase
come next week,
all her boyfriends

disappointments—
does not need another?
Perhaps I misunderstand...

Fool! You've known
this feeling in your bones
and lump in your throat

often enough, old as days
of puppy-love—it is over.
No need for her to say the word.

Moving On

She asked herself why
not?—burning a few boats might
at least light the sky.

Opening Time

I am remembering
how we ducked the wet,
warmed ourselves

in a pub in York—
oak beams
graffitied in chalk,

things like
"Heard of the dyslexic
pimp?

last week
he invested
in a warehouse."

O woman
who shared that day,
I will not forget.

Will forget the one
on the next stool
this morning going on

about the secret
of her looks:
"An hour stroking

salad cream
through the scalp,
almonds for the face,

yoga for the upholstery,
egg yoke and brandy
to keep the eyes bright."

Your ghost weaves
from the CD
disguised as

Mississippi creole
singing what we'd told each other;
"You don't owe me your soul."

The barmaid calls after
a regular
who is leaving early:

"If you die
on the way home
don't forget to phone us."

I'm winking at her
and at the notice
behind the bar

Those drinking
to forget
kindly pay in advance.

Romance

Summer afternoons
mostly spent
reading on the roof.

He became a fixture
the squirrels
soon ignored.

Some days a banging
from below:
he'd peer

over the guttering,
not answer unless
her bicycle

leant against
the maple-
devil's-horn-sycamore.

Kate! her smile beyond compare—
ineffably open, blithe,
yet subtle as sly can be.

Cornucopia

1

In the way
I will never know
where you went

it's likely
I never knew
where you

really
came from—
absent

yet present
all these years:
so it was, so it is.

2

As I roved out one morning
none the worse for wear

you flitted in and out of mind
like finches in woodland.

A crowd of finches is called 'a charm'—
did I ever tell you the plural?

Their singing is not birdsong
their song is called 'a twinkle'.

So many things I forgot to say
yet you gave me a cornucopia:

embroidered on the ass of your jeans
the heart is deceitful above all things.

"What, dearest, does that mean?"
"Read your Bible:

Jeremiah,
seventeen, verse nine."

You said of an alley's rain-glossed cobbles
"richly toned as dying leaves"

and in Glasgow you dragged me to view
a Margaret Macdonald Mackintosh—

her painting haunting as its title
'O ye, All ye that walk in Willow Wood'.

Adrift

Sure as cats cry in the night
lust at first sight will come back
amusing, tickling the spirit
a month or two, a bare week
until she tells you "This is fake!"—
or maybe you'll be first to wake
and say "Who's this in my bed?"
politely kiss her cheek,
"Sorry, lady, my mistake",
offer coffee, throw her out.
You might think of this or that
or someone years, years back
when blessings sparked your luck
yet you managed to lose
the woman whose eyes mattered—
brown? Chestnut, yellow flecks.

Dusky Curls
after the Sanskrit

I know well
the talk of philosophers
in ivory towers,
of priests who've prayed
away their youth;
I listen to the salt
whisperings of you,
murmur of colours
as we lie near sleep—
little wise words
little witty words
honeyed with eagerness
wanton as water.

I know well
larks rising at morning,
the scent of thyme,
great blue mountains,
gorse fires in valleys,
I know strange eyes
and hands like butterflies.

I know well
the savour of life,
lift goblets high
at feasts—
our small, small
soon to be
forgotten time—
the loveliest pourings
pourings from the soul,
your sidelong glances.

I know well
the flickering
of powdery lids
that will
not live forever—
keep me this while
in your wild eyes—
slim body
wearied with
the weariness of joy,
little red
flowers of your breasts,
wet crimson lips.

I know well
small men chatter
about you in bars,
small men who are
slaves to gold and silver
who buy and sell
through eyes
crinkled with fat—
yet none of these
merchant princes
has led you to his bed.

I know well
chestnut eyes
can caress like silk,
sad laughing eyes
whose lids make such sweet
shadows when they close,
yet it's only another
beautiful look of yours—
I love a scented mouth,
curving hair

subtle as smoke,
lively fingers—
moons growing
in fingernails
painted pearl
or emerald.

I know well
your hand on my hair,
your hair tinted
by the neap-tide moon,
your body breaking
over mine
making love—
dark one,
before you
my heart was buried
alive in snow.

I know well
night falling
and a grey-haired lover
on the breasts of day,
incense
of your lips—
plaited hair
ropes of herbs—
or, worn loose,
dusky curls
tapping against cheeks
of magnolia flowers—
whitest soft parchment
where I have written
stanzas of kisses.

Heavy wine—
a reeling pirate bee
taking nectar
from a tulip—
I know well
chestnut eyes
opening, closing
as I drink
from your mouth.

PART THREE

Lakeside

Creek Feather,
sit again on the toes

of the hawk-beaver tree,
tell me midnight stories:

how lunar touches
make beauties of hags,

gleaming dice
of warriors' bones;

or say again the saga
of your Greyhound travels,

San Joaquin
to Wounded Knee,

how you watched
the morning:

wispy clouds—
paint-starved brushstrokes;

or say nothing as night
pauses between

the leaves, the lake
and the whippoorwill.

Ghost Dance
i.m. Chief Little Wing

God men say
when die go sky

through pearly gates
where river flow

God men say
when die we fly

just like eagle
hawk and crow—

maybe, maybe so—
I don't know.

You found out
whether there is a tavern

over the wall or through
a gap in the fence of heaven

whether the mystery of women
is no more than

men's wild imaginings—
I wish you'd talk

instead of ghosting as a grace-note
on breeze through wind-chimes.

Sketch

Small girl on the beach
plays a new game

stands at the sea's edge
arms outstretched

fingers crossed
hands dangling

and I follow her stare—
cormorant on a rock

sketch in charcoal
drying its plumage

splayed wings black
as twists of liquorice

the bird flaps
drops its arms to dive

the girl on the beach
folds her wings.

Weeshy

Five years old,
   another country:
we were sweethearts
   and the sea
an old tambourine.

A door opened
   on a dazzle
drying the mat
   and yesterday's sand
in your sandals;
   down the path
past the lighthouse
   ebb-tide turned
ocean into rock-pools;
   the shingle
was shushed maracas
   of rolling pebbles and shells—
fiddle-head tops of waves,
   song in the surf.

For Katie Nicola Madden

You of the rich darkest brown hair.
eyes the bright brown of chestnuts,
thirteen years on this Earth:

born in the month
of the fruiting of the elder tree—
elder sacred to the wren

and the winter solstice;
child of the Christmas month,
Nicola, the wren remains

king of the birds— as you are queen
of whatever skies you carry
in the privacy of your heart.

Sibling
for Dave

Mother came home
showing off my brother—
I bided time
until it was alone,

fed it a sandwich
of clay and worm,
privet leaves for bread;
the brat survived.

So goes family legend,
yet, now and then,
I am inclined
to re-imagine

that sandwich a gauche
manner of greeting—
clueless go at communing
with the creature.

Four A.M.

Wolf hour, false dawn.
I stare at my trees
through a light shower.

Not real raindrops
more a shimmer
of shiny new pins

recalling estimations:
how many teetering angels
acrobat on a pinhead—

they are crashing
to earth, the hushed
Oh Shits of spilled angels.

All night, blocked from sleep,
hooked on a sentence
in a book on Nostradamus:

"There is something slightly comic
in the notion of a basin
of water composing verses."

I am thinking how divination
by gazing at a bowl of water
was common in antiquity;

how, in sympathetic magic,
rocking a pail violently
churns up a storm on the lake.

Yet, a versifying basin—
unlike, say, a babbling brook—
strains my faith

in miracles...
Fuddled from lack of sleep,
I stare out at thickening rain

clouding dawn back into night,
serious rain conversing with roots
as I think cats and dogs

but mainly of how the Japanese
in their painting use rain so quietly
it's like a downpouring of light.

Searching for an Answer
from the Bulgarian of Kristin Dimitrova

I asked the sky
"Why am I here?"
It swallowed
my words & waited for more.

I wondered
what else I could add.

I asked the earth
"Why am I here?"
It shrugged its mountains.

I asked the fire
"Why am I here?"
Busily crackling
it did not hear a word.

I went to the well
& asked the water
"Why am I here?"
"Come down to me
& I will tell you."

"Actually" I said
"I was only asking."

A Sofia Notebook
for Elena

Before you strolled across the lobby
to our pure-chance encounter

I knew few words; probably
mispronounced, or out of place
— like *maika*, meaning 'mother'.

Luggage lost in Prague,
travelogue of smaller disasters...

I went roaming markets and alleys,
put my ear to a ground-swell
of voices, mused awhile on the fabled

city of Shinar, its tower called Babel;
turned corners where the wind from the West

had forgotten my name, my name growing
strange to myself, shedding its baggage...

Before you walked across
that hotel lobby to share an ashtray
I was literate as an infant.

In the twinkling of an eye
our exchanges begin.

*

As we drink tankards of Kamenitza
in the yard of the bar we nickname
'Tavern of Lunatics Smiling',
a starling comes to dine.
Hops fearlessly on the table,
gives you, gives me, a beady
appraising sideways look, a nod.
And takes a leftover, a big crumb,
flutters a leap to the ground
where she feeds the morsel, beak-to-beak,
mouth-to-mouth, to her mate—
her mate, no fledgling;
this pair could be man and wife.

**

Sauntering streets with you
I am careful, focused, tonight—
need to store everything.
We pass a strange house,
sign above its door I can't comprehend
— "Tell me, what's that in English?"
— "It says Sisters of Mercy."
— "Ah... so it's a coven of nuns?"
— "*Ne!* You fool, *Sisters of Mercy*
is knocking shop, is famous brothel."
Walking the streets with you
I try taking everything in—
the swings in the park, that clump of cedars,
matte-grey tower blocks built by Soviets —
anything memory might want
to find the trail back...
Yes, I am dropping rivulets of rice,
chalking imaginary signs on trees,
to hold onto, go over, our paths.
Fool! Old enough to have learned
there is no return to now.

***

Freight Depot... it explains why
there are no quays in Sofia...
I sleep sixteen floors
above the shunting yards.
Through the night, banging of wagon
on wagon, their screechings over the points.
Not a bother: it's a noise familiar
from years ago— so much so
that their clattering percussion
mingling with night-thoughts of you
is just another lullaby.
From the high balcony at sunrise,
godlike, I watch the insect shunters
fly-shunting great coils of freights;
remember how it was, *how it still is,*
arcane knacks for marshalling trains.
Now I look beyond it all,
watch from my light-drenched eyrie
morning stroking the blue mountains—
before descending to heaven on earth,
our tryst at 'The Lunatics' at noon.

****

Among the cars
the gypsyman's cart
crawls...
The drovers sit forward on planks,
we sit in the shade counting
the donkeys to pass the time:
score one point for the unadorned ones,
two for those with scarlet tassels.
I feel I'm witnessing the drawn-out twilight
of an era... muse on shorter time,
how swiftly our blessèd days are passing.
You haul me back, saying
"Your turn, who next shall we toast?"
I trawl time for the right ghosts—come up with
"Bulgaria being his Illyria,
we'll raise a polite glass to Shakespeare;
toast also oracular Orpheus
for here is his country, ancient Thrace."

*****

Your apartment, I stretch on the bed.
You put a tape on
of swirling, almost dervish music,
leave the room and return naked.
Dear heart, how like you this?
I whisper "Come here to me."
"Ne," you say, "Now I want to dance."
You begin slow, toes in the air, leg-stretching;
arms above your head in flame-shape—
soon go into frenzy with the frenzied strings.
Too much for me: only thing to do—
get up and join you, whirling, whirling,
spinning until we collapse. Kiss of life.

******

Sofia... named for Saint Sofia:
her church built here, sixth century,
by a Byzantine emperor.
We walk to her towering monument—
Sofia, you do not seem
too happy on your column,
your dress blown out behind—
wind flaring petticoats of bronze.
Something else, deeper. does not fit:
not just that you appear like no saint I know,
no sister to plaster ones back home;
your bearing— more goddess-warrior.
Who are you? Again I stare:
your right hand holds a laurel crown,
poorly weathered, looks more like a wreath—
yes, in Bulgarian, Death is feminine.
On your left shoulder, what seems like an owl:
bird of wisdom— Sofia, could you be
a disguised *Sophia*, Spirit of Wisdom?
Your face is masked, painted over in gold—
honestly, you look awful.
Come down, I will introduce you
to my girlfriend: together we will find
the gilding cretin who so messed up your face;
we shall let him down gently
into a bath of boiling oil.

****

Today the watch you gifted me
hiccups and stops. I wind it on.
Resuscitated no more than a minute
it hiccups again. I wind it—
this time, it stays ticking...
                    All afternoon,
like monitoring a sick child,
I check that its second-hand still moves.
A day old, two year guarantee,
whatever ails it can be mended?
Repair might take hours, perhaps weeks—
too many moments out of my sight...
Thumbing through the booklet you stuffed
in my pocket, the one with the vendor's stamp,
I learn what's meant by 'Automatic':
it needs body-warmth to keep going,
too long off the wrist it stops,
needs my pulse— even when maybe
you don't mean to, you surprise me.

****

Always you surprise me but never more
than when you announced, "Your number is nine.'
I've read enough to know this is so,
allow myself superstitious pride in it—
three times three, magic mystical number.
Nines are rare and I was only guessing
in answering, "It takes one to know one."
You smiled, I smiled: two nines are eighteen;
in numerology, that is nine.
You went on: "Your colours are grey and black—
you know, silvery grey with dark bits
like a feather shed from a pigeon."
I know the colours of the moon—
white, red, and black— but not my own.
Perhaps they alter with moods and seasons.
Always easier to spy
colours of others— yours: silver and black...
Our days nearing their end, alone I wander
streets around the bulbous golden
onion domes of Alexandra Nevsky,
searching for the right gift— find a bracelet
of silver with studs of black onyx:
silver, for you are silver-tongued,
black for your storm of dusky curls
and eyes the bluish black of ripe olives.
The jeweller, looking at me askance,
goes with my wishes: removes the tenth stud.

****

I notice the flowers on our table,
on this the day before I have to leave,
are green and white and orange:
emblem of home, eerie symbolism.
My fingers playing with yours, I ask
what is the meaning of Bulgaria's
horizontally striped tricolour—
"White at top, that is for peace;
green in middle, that is the land;
red, at end, for no more bloodshed."
I salute, *sláinte,*
you clink glasses, *zdrave.*
And another for the road—the road
is surely dipsomaniac...
Yes, today, let us be frivolous.

73

Printed in the United Kingdom
by Lightning Source UK Ltd.
113426UKS00001B/499-573

9 781904 556541